Business Smarts Lead

To

Business Success

"Obtain the keys to business success by knowing what you want, going after it, keeping it and managing it all."

By

Kevin D. Regular, CPCM

DEDICATION

I am dedicating this book to my wonderful family. Dinia, my business savvy wife; Kinchazsa, my daughter and spiritual voice of reason; and Kevin Jr., my forever entrepreneuring son. Together, they have been my pillar through the many years. Without family, there is nothing. Nothing and no one can replace the inspiration that I have had every day for the last 26 years since my life has been blessed with these beacons of light.

Also, I am dedicating this book to my resilient mother, Mrs. Kattie M. Regular, and my late father, Mr. W.D. Regular. Words cannot express how these two molded me into the man that I am today. My mother is without a doubt the strongest woman I know and I have been blessed to have acquired her skills in being detail oriented and unrelenting in doing things the right way.

My late father blessed me with being the intellect that I am today. His ability to decipher complicated topics and his gift of communicating have forever emboldened me and for that, I will be forever thankful.

As you read my teachings on business, please understand that personal success should always be first and all other successes will only be sweeter.

Husband, Father and Son,

Kevin

INTRODUCTION

Business is about four things. Knowing what you want, going after what you want, keeping what you have, and managing it all. Within all four of those areas, there are rules to follow to be a business success. In the next thirteen chapters, we will explore what's needed to have a clear business vision, aptitude to go after business, tools to retain business, and skills to manage people to build your business.

Corporate managers and business owners alike must possess the skills necessary to grow and build their professions. The areas to be discussed in this book not only build the foundations for business success, but these rules are proven and timeless in having a strong business intelligence. In my experience and experiences of many professionals, true life business exposure is the real classroom for learning. In the chapters to follow, real true experiences have been captured to provide smart lessons in making decisions and avoiding pitfalls that many professionals encounter.

This book is for entrepreneurs, senior management and corporate executives. There is a benefit from the core thoughts of beginning with a solid business vision to understanding the critical issues of management.

Business is competitive and it rightly should be. The question is, "What are the fundamental attributes to be a serious and strong competitor?" This book is a straight in-your-face common-sense approach to real business strategy.

CONTENTS

Chapter One - "Know The Company Vision To See Business Develop"

Chapter Two - "Business Development"

Chapter Three - "Pursuing Business"

Chapter Four - "Negotiation"

Chapter Five - "Contract Importance"

Chapter Six - "Risk Mitigation"

Chapter Seven - "Understanding Your Competition"

Chapter Eight - "Peril At Your Competition's Hand"

Chapter Nine - "Innovation V.S. Stagnation"

Chapter Ten - "The Importance of Diversifying Business"

Chapter Eleven - "Value Driven"

Chapter Twelve - "How Does Your Organizational Performance Impact Business Development?"

Chapter Thirteen - "Managing Your People For Success"

CHAPTER ONE

KNOW THE COMPANY VISION TO SEE BUSINESS DEVELOP

Obtaining more accounts and higher profits should not be enough to keep your business in existence. When your business was being built there should have been mission, objective and vision statements written as your foundation. As time goes by, these crucial foundations of your business are forgotten, and the ultimate mission of more money takes their place.

Remember, most businesses were created from a thought of providing more value. The money should be an indicator of your efforts in providing the value that your business was intended to provide.

This is where we get lost as business owners. Increased profits should be a goal and a gauge to understand if your business is providing value; however, profits can lead to a blurred vision of which direction you should be taking your business. For example, if your company produces a truly valuable product that is based on making the lives of others comfortable in the health industry, it would be completely out of vision to set your prices to where the costs are so exorbitantly high that those very clients that your vision was set to help cannot afford your products.

To have a clear direction for your business, you must think of a need that is relevant in today's marketplace and have a plan to evolve your business over the years while taking into consideration economic and market changes. A vision should be more than just where you want your company to be, but your vision should be a well-thought-out goal taking into consideration obstacles along the way. Remember, the idea here is to have a clear vision and not be blind.

Before beginning my management consulting company, I gave a lot of thought to what exactly it was that I wanted to do. I first began thinking about consulting over 15 years ago while obtaining my bachelor's degree in business management. So, in understanding the length of time it took for me to begin consulting, it is easier to understand how I thoroughly thought what was needed to add value as a business consultant. Once I began to write my business plan, I considered my vision meticulously. The best advice I can give when developing a business vision is to keep it solid and direct to the point. If anyone reads your vision and still has questions as to what you are trying to accomplish, you don't have a clear business vision.

CHAPTER TWO

BUSINESS DEVELOPMENT

Business development from a capability perspective begins with understanding what your company needs to become and stay competitive. By this, I mean having the right people, processes, and tools in place. This is simply understanding your needs based decision-making and capture planning processes. A business must first analyze and understand its strengths, weaknesses, and future vision, then do a needs-based analysis (when buying) and capture planning (when selling) to position itself to be more competitive.

If you are a buyer in business-to-business, you must conduct a needs-based analysis to understand where your company is in the buying process and what the end goal is in purchasing the product or service needed to make your business strategically strong in the marketplace. Similarly, if you are selling you should be conducting the proper capture plans to fully vet the pros and cons of providing a bid to your customers as well as thoroughly understanding the business that you are going after.

Needs-based decision-making is a process businesses go through when there is room for improvement and this improvement is accomplished by adding a competitive edge through purchasing whatever is needed to gain that edge. The main strategy here is to thoroughly understand what your business needs to build your strengths whether that is partnering with another business or adding to what you offer.

Capture planning is having the right steps in place to win business. It is a known fact that before a customer places a request for a bid in the marketplace, the customer has a good idea who they will be buying from. You, as a business owner, need to thoroughly understand the market and be proactive in putting proposals together that totally answer a customer's need. This is done by involving the right people before the customer's solicitation until the submission of your proposal. Once your proposals start winning business, you will become well known in the market and obtain more business.

Business development is a combination of several groups of people within your organization whom all have expertise in a specific subject area. No one is greater or more important than the other, but through a team, the entire group is highly performing.

Your business development team at a minimum should consist of senior management, direct salespersons, project management and proposal management. By having these persons involved in the beginning, there is a clear understanding of the end vision of what the business development goal should be. This list of people includes the decision-makers, front-line staff, project experts and support staff.

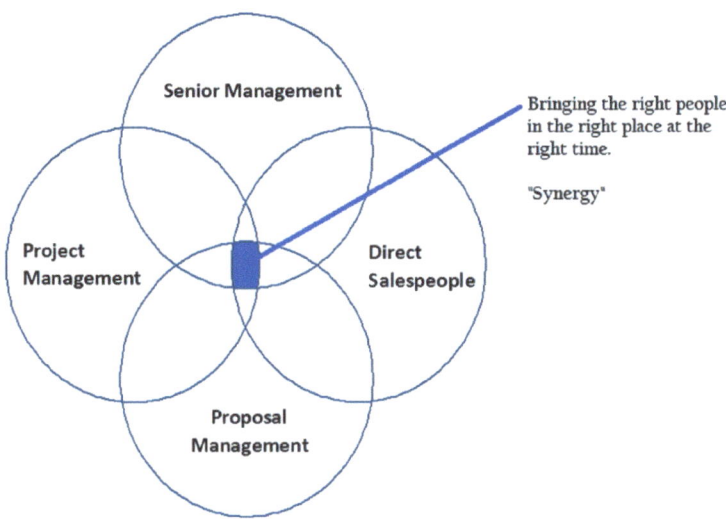

There are different steps to be taken depending upon if your business is business-to-business or business-to-end consumer. In either case, there are some similar end-goals to keep in mind.

For strategic purposes, understanding what your business needs to maintain its competitiveness begins with understanding market trends from a past, present and future approach. In addition to understanding market trends, you must always consider what society sees as truly valuable. Always understand when you produce a service or product with true market value, business success will follow.

CHAPTER THREE

PURSUING BUSINESS

What keeps the lights on at your business? Is it what's drafted in your business plan, mission, or vision statements? Maybe on a broader scale it can be. However, on a daily, hourly, and monthly basis, finding business that is value driven, cost effective, supported by your knowledge capabilities and fits your business model is the business that is going to keep your bills paid, lights on and revenue coming in.

A business is only as valuable as the value that it creates. Your clients will keep coming back if they have a need to have what you provide. Building your client base will grow exponentially if you provide a valuable product or service and the word of mouth generates interest for your product or service.

Regarding cost effectiveness, all aspects of how you produce, market, and provide your products or services must be taken into consideration and carefully understood. In my past business ventures, I have developed high quality products, which entailed costs that had to be rolled into the end product. When this is the case, as a business owner you must understand that the more costs rolled into the production of what you're selling must be passed down to your buyers.

In determining end costs for your products and services, many new businesses fail to account for all costs appropriately. Smaller new businesses are good at accounting for the actual costs for goods sold but fail to account for the labor involved. This is especially true for product-oriented small businesses. To be fair to yourself, never forget to take into fact your time spent developing your end product. This also includes the time staff spend in production of your end products and services as well.

Understand who works for you and quickly realize if you have the right people for the job. Even if you are the only employee in your business, be honest with yourself and ask the question "Do I have the knowledge and skills to operate my business properly?" This is crucial because if the answer is no, you need to either get out of the business or plan to outsource. There is nothing wrong with outsourcing, but you must realize that this is an extra cost of doing business. On the other hand, as a business owner who has staff, you must make sure that you have the right people and that you foster the knowledge and talent that they possess to pursue new business.

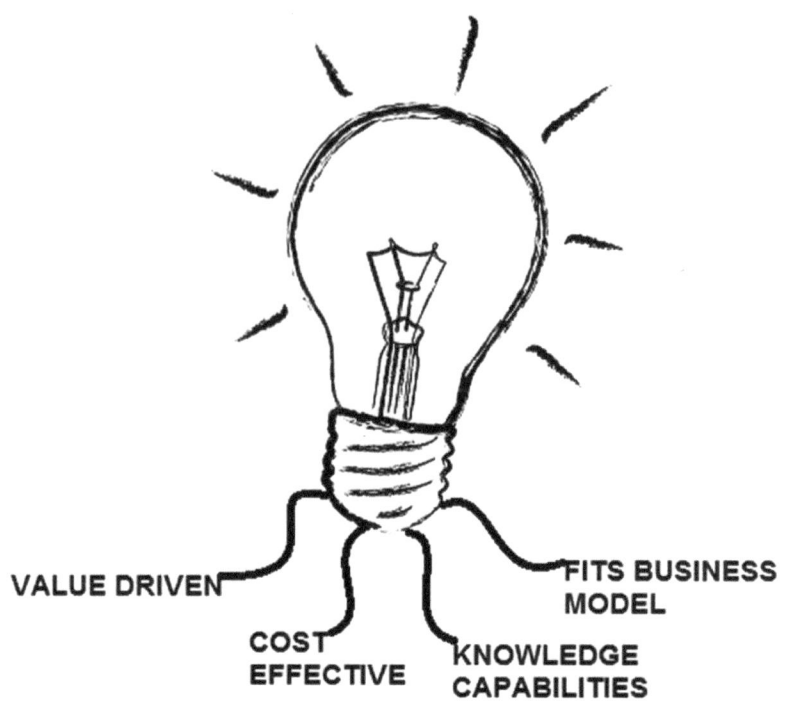

Adding value, maintaining your costs, having the right knowledge and staying aligned with your business model will keep your business performing.

Pursuing business is more than just going after business. You must make sure that what you go after fits your business model. What this means is your pursuit of business should align with your strategies outlined in your business plan. This does not mean you should never diversify what you offer as a business (discussed later), but you should make sure your business pursuits are what's good for your business at the time that you pursue new business.

CHAPTER FOUR

NEGOTIATION

Your win and their loss? Sharing high-fives with your team after the deal? This may be the case after a high stake's negotiation, but do you really realize who the winner is? If the other side of the table was truly valuable to your business, but did not feel that the outcome was fair, they will eventually realize that doing business with you is not good business at all. They will never do business with you again or if they do, they will bargain much harder the next time causing a stalemate or even worse, in your case, a bad deal.

This happens far too many times when we view a business deal as just a deal and don't think of long-term relationships. Think of it this way, business-to-business networking is just as important as personal networking because your business reputation as a business owner must be done with integrity. Having a good reputation will foster business relationships on an ongoing basis creating growth or at least strengthening bonds that will lead to growth.

To avoid the pitfall of the "I got over on them" mentality, there are some very basic rules to abide by well before negotiating begins. In fact, these simple rules should be known at the outset of a decision to buy or sell.

1. Know the business of your business. This may sound simple but often negotiators sitting at the table are not totally connected to the business goal. Nor are the people making decisions aware of industry factors impacting potential areas of the deal.

   Before the decision to sell or purchase, all key areas of the organization should be involved in the reasons for the deal. Depending on how large or small the organization, the minimum key stakeholders such as senior management, program management, credit, legal, and contract management should be on board. Getting more than needed input before the key decisions are made will ensure that when negotiating begins, the entire organization will be in tune with the ultimate end goal.

   Having a clear understanding of why the deal is being done will also make it easier to agree on certain concessions if those need to be made during negotiations. There will always be a need to have sidebar conversations during negotiations but having a solid vision before getting started will display the negotiation team as a unified team.

2. Understand your strengths, weaknesses, opportunities, and threats (S.W.O.T). This will take some in-depth internal realizations, which will include visiting with other team members. A good way to do this is to create a skills matrix of various skills sets in your organization and rank those skills placing weights or values on those skills in relation to the deal being sought. This will not only cause your organization to know how to negotiate but ultimately allow your organization to determine if the deal should be pursued.

   Organizations change rapidly so conducting a S.W.O.T analysis should be done on a regular basis. Team members change on a regular basis, organizational structure changes as well as the culture of the organization. All of these have an impact on the strength or weakness of an organization.

3. In addition to understanding your organization's strengths, weaknesses, opportunities, and threats, <u>know your counterparty's</u> S.W.O.T as well. It is amazing how many times an organization goes into a negotiation without understanding the capabilities on the other side of the table. This is a very big mistake. Just understanding the counterpart's position will lead to a more satisfied negotiation for both your company and the

counterparty. You will understand what the needs and goals are of the counterparty, which leads to the next topic of understanding – the counterpart's end goals.

4. Every business in a negotiation has an end goal in mind. It's just as important to understand your counterpart's goals as it is to understand your own. Keep in mind all goals are not based on monetary factors. In fact, many goals can be based on other areas such as delivery schedule, quality, and relationship.

   Always keep in mind that negotiating is a form of relationship building. In other words, you are there to provide something that your counterpart needs, and they are there to provide you with something that you need. If you don't understand and meet the end goals of your counterpart, they will feel unsatisfied in the relationship and choose not to do business with you and more likely feel the need to do business with someone else.

5. This brings us to the last but important topic of discussion, which is to truly understand your business goal in a negotiating situation. Have a well-thought-out plan before entering into any negotiation. Without a plan, it is very possible that a

counterparty will take advantage of the situation. Feel confident in why you are sitting in the room across the table. Be specific about what you want out of the business relationship. Uncertainty or appearing uncertain will later lead to ambiguities in your contract (if the deal is done!) and even possible litigation down the road. Remember being specific is terrific especially when you know what you want to walk away from the table with.

Remember, negotiating is an art form, and it may take a while to perfect the craft; however, with a great team and excellent direction, the pitfalls of losing deals can be overcome. Whether you have a big business or small business, deals can be negotiated and won. The "win-win" phrase is not only a phrase and should be sought out in every deal. Relationships in all business negotiations should be one of the key outcomes of negotiating.

In business development, particularly business-to-business development, a business owner must have the skills to negotiate. In fact, proper negotiation falls into both business development and risk mitigation. Terms of a deal are always part of developing business. The commercial terms of a deal such as price, style, quantity and delivery period are often negotiated outside of the general terms and conditions of a deal, but both are equally important in developing a deal and controlling potential risks.

CHAPTER FIVE

CONTRACT IMPORTANCE

When most people think of contracts they think of traps, attorneys, lawsuits, and other stressful thoughts that make most want to avoid the idea of being involved in a contract. The truth is a contract can be the simplest part of conducting business and not to mention the most important. Let's be honest, we are involved in contracts and contractual negotiations in our daily lives whether they be with our families or business-related concerns.

The only time we think negatively of contracts is when we really do not understand what we value out of a situation. The thought of entering a situation that will become a conflict is the reason why we feel contracts should be used. This is more of a safety precaution or to overt possible risks. Having clarity of what all parties value before, during, and after the contract is written will always minimize the negative feelings of having a contractual arrangement.

A contract is not a tool to be used to make one party feel as though they have been used, but a contract should be a tool that says, "We have come to a mutual decision and one that will be beneficial for both of us". As human beings, we have become frightened of commitment and what a contract states is that we are truly committed to upholding our end of the deal. Regardless of how anyone sees it, a marriage is a contract, your relationship with your kids is a contract, and your life with God is a contract. These are commitments that speak to your character when you uphold your end of the deal.

Understand that being a business owner or individual entering a business decision takes thought and consideration. When considering that next business venture or any decision that is a commitment, take time to step back and think of the relationship that the decision will create. Realize that the agreement that you are committing yourself to can be a long-lasting one and one that you will enjoy as well as provide enjoyment for the party on the other side of the deal.

Contracts and agreements do not have to be death sentences or "I got over on you" scenarios. Creating a binding agreement should be well-thought out, reciprocal, and an overall benefit to everyone involved. Create long-lasting relationships that reflect how differences and similarities come together in a contract for success.

CHAPTER SIX

RISK MITIGATION

Business risk mitigation applies to many different areas of your business. When most people think of risks they think of the "not-so-great" result of making a decision. They think of taking a gamble and hoping it pays off. While this thought of risk is true, in the business world risks often don't have to do with taking gambles but instead simply <u>failing to plan</u> to avoid risks. In a sense, failing to plan is a gamble as well. At any rate, business risk mitigation is a necessary business action that should be an ever-existing tool in properly operating a business.

To list a few areas in risk management, the following are good rules to follow:

1. <u>Reduce the possibility</u> of experiencing the risk. This includes having a thorough review of project details before starting the sales or purchase decision, which involves including key stakeholders in the beginning. This also includes practicing good contract review and negotiation techniques.

2. <u>Avoiding the risk</u> is the process of foregoing projects or business activity where there is an absolute known risk. In this instance, there needs to be a risk versus reward analysis

communicated at all levels of management to ensure avoiding the risk is the best alternative.

3. <u>Lessen the impact</u> of the potential risk becoming a reality. In this instance, there should be thorough contingency planning done as well as cost measurements to ensure there is minimal impact to ongoing business initiatives and low impact to revenue.

4. <u>Transferring the risk</u> or "spreading" the risk across multiple parties such as partnerships and insurance is an alternative. As always, there should be extensive analysis to justify a partnership situation. Having insurance may not only be a good idea but may be mandatory depending on the type of business.

5. <u>Absorbing risk</u> has some similarities to avoiding risk in that there should be careful consideration to the health of your business to understand the impact of a risk-related situation. Risk analysis should be done by completing the following steps:

    - Evaluating the business' historical performance.
    - Looking at Industry trends.
    - Reviewing your company's overall financial strength.

- Taking into consideration the knowledge of personnel.

Controlling risks will lead to more profitability and longevity of your business.

CHAPTER SEVEN

UNDERSTANDING YOUR COMPETITION

Always know one thing when it comes down to your competitors and that is the ones to pay attention to the most are the ones that are watching your every step. These are the people that follow your business on social media, subscribe to any updates you provide and the ones that will set up a meeting with you in the disguise of developing a business partnership.

I once was contacted by a business owner who reached out as a so-called opportunity for a "synergy" moment between our two companies working together. Indeed, we met, and the meeting appeared to have been a fruitful relationship. In fact, this business owner suggested I provide a proposal to assist him in reviewing some of his business processes. Of course, I provided a proposal in hopes that this would not only be potential business but also an opportunity for a greater partnership.

Unfortunately, after my thoroughly drafted proposal was given to the business owner, I never heard from him again. This was not due to a failure on my end to properly follow up. In fact, follow-up meetings were scheduled to discuss my proposal and confirm that the intent of the business project was captured. Every measure was taken to ensure that a solid business relationship was established. However, after repeated unanswered phone calls and sent emails, I was given the cold shoulder. Was this because my proposal was too expensive? Or was there never any intention on the business owner's end to establish a business relationship?

Since that meeting and my proposal offer, I've had a lot of time to contemplate the entire event and have come to an eye-opening conclusion. Someone who sees you as potential competition will use any tactic necessary to explore your methods including meeting with you in the disguise of doing business. It wasn't that my offer was too expensive because all seasoned professionals know that there's an opportunity to negotiate a proposal. Treat your competition or potential competition as an opposing team. Never, never expose your playbook even when providing a proposal and keep your closest strategies close. Those who pretend to do business with you can be wolves in sheep clothing.

Those who pretend to be your business partner can be wolves in sheep clothing.

Competition in today's marketplace is extremely strong and this is actually a good thing. Clients have the option to choose from a number of businesses for products and services. Although there are still some areas of big business where there is a monopolistic trend occurring, especially in technology, many small businesses are keeping the true definition of free market society alive. This is where entrepreneurs are so extremely important to real business.

CHAPTER EIGHT

PERIL AT YOUR COMPETITION'S HAND

Just because you've never had an issue with another business in the past does not mean a soured relationship will not create a fierce business opponent. Always think of the potential risks of doing business even when the business relationship is good. Not to be a pessimist, but partnerships and teaming arrangements are great when they work, but these same arrangements can be damning if there is fallout between your company and the company that has learned your every move. This is where confidentiality agreements come into play.

Generally known as another form of a contractual document, confidentiality agreements or CAs, as many call them, are binding agreements that ensure your business methods or processes are prevented from being shared to third parties and typically have an expiration once the business arrangement is complete.

Another binding document to keep your business information from getting in the wrong hands when shared with another business is a proprietary information agreement or PIA. This is a document that is executed when your business information, such as trade secrets or specialized processes that you use are shared with another business and you want a binding agreement to enforce your proprietary information from being exposed. Very similar to a confidentiality agreement, a proprietary information agreement is binding and enforceable in a court of law.

These are a couple of business tools to use to ensure that if your business requires partnering to expand your business potential, you can have a legal basis to protect what's most important to you, which is your business methods and processes.

CHAPTER NINE

INNOVATION V.S. STAGNATION

If you've paid attention to businesses large and small, you've noticed the ones that have been around for a while compared to the ones that are no longer around. There are two words that you need to know that make the difference between longevity and hindrance, which are innovation and stagnation. An innovative company continuously seeks change and embraces change. On the other hand, a company that is stagnating fears change, possibly from a history of successes or a history of "just being good enough".

Over the many years in my professional career, I have had the opportunity to work with and for corporations that are innovative and stagnate. This has been a blessing. The companies that were innovative invited input regularly from their employees and the companies that were stagnate shunned input from their employees. In addition to shunning input, these stagnate companies had the tendency to withhold learned knowledge by not sharing that knowledge. I've learned that this type of corporate culture typically had individuals that either were too busy to pass down learned knowledge or afraid of losing their jobs to younger and newer talent. Unfortunately, the latter was the more common reason for these companies' stagnation and lack of progress.

Ultimately, it's everyone's responsibility to champion the organization's embracing of innovation. Employees will know better ways and methods of conducting business more efficiently, but without the support of management to generate new ideas, employees will be reluctant to share their ideas.

I like to call innovation a "mold breaking process". Even if the mold that you have has created a beautiful end product, there should be a point where you evaluate what you have been doing and try a newer and better way. This is where creative experimentation takes place. Just like before there were aircraft, the Wright Brothers exercised creative experimentation to do something that had never been done. Today, the value that the aircraft has will forever exist and has changed the entire world. Innovation at its core is a life-changing concept.

What makes an organization continue to thrive over many years as others fall by the wayside? Does your organization know what it takes to continuously be competitive? The answer to both is simple, which is review how things are done in your organization on a regular basis. Challenge your processes and look for areas of improvement as if the processes can always be done better. Although this thought is quite simple, most organizations do not practice it. In fact, the mainstream thought has been "If it isn't broken, don't fix it". The issue does not have to be that business has come to a complete halt. However, reviewing processes will always uncover better methods, especially in aged processes.

Not tearing old processes down and rebuilding newer and better ones leads to one common tragedy, which is COMPLACENCY. Yes, complacency, the evil word that has destroyed empires, organizations, and the most brilliant individuals throughout history. To avoid the pitfalls of failing to apply process improvements, let's look at the main reasons why continuously reviewing your processes and improving them will lead to a more competitive organization.

1. <u>Technology Changes:</u> With the changes in technology, efficiency is the ultimate reason why organizations must embrace technological advances. I have seen many organizations use old platforms created years ago, as opposed to upgrading to newer and efficient platforms. Not upgrading causes two main issues that organizations fail to realize. The first is inefficiency of co-workers using these old platforms. Valuable time is often lost when inefficient programs are used by staff. The second issue is risk exposure. Many outdated technologies do not have the same risk mitigating advances that new programs have, which have resulted over years of learning and improving.
2. <u>People Changes:</u> With the changing in mindsets among the incoming workforce, younger generations have a different skill set and work ethic than other generations. This creates an opportunity in that the new workforce understands the value of being coachable. Coaching the workforce to question the current processes will only add value to the organization. Many different and innovative ideas can come from allowing the incoming generation to think and express their thoughts. Encourage creative thinking and a boundaryless environment.

3. <u>Waste Elimination:</u> A major positive that has always been a part of process improvement is to eliminate unnecessary and time-consuming activities. To enhance processes does not mean to apply more processes. In fact, it's just the opposite. Where employees' time can be spent re-thinking and challenging processes there should not be redundant work activities. Time is money and eliminating waste will only lead to profitability.

4. <u>Business Alignment:</u> The business vision of yesterday will not always be the business vision of today or tomorrow. Constantly reviewing how your organization's processes are conducted will ensure that the way things are being done are in alignment with where the company is trying to be. The way that things are done on every level of management and employee activity must be focused and aligned with the organization's current business vision.

5. <u>Competitive Advantage:</u> A professional athlete trains to obtain overall better athleticism and the process it takes to get there includes various activities that can be outside that athlete's main sport. However, every athlete knows that he or she has a competitive advantage in their main sport. In having said this,

focus your organizational processes to sharpen your competitive advantage as an organization. Do not have processes in place that will never complement your main strengths in the business that you are focusing on. A service-oriented business may use some processes meant for a product-oriented business, but focus should be placed on processes meant for the line of business that the organization is involved in. Change is difficult but necessary to maintain a competitive edge. Instill thinking throughout your organization to routinely challenge why, what, where, how and even who in terms of daily business activities. Without a doubt, there will eventually be some constructive conversations surrounding process improvements.

CHAPTER TEN

THE IMPORTANCE OF DIVERSIFYING YOUR BUSINESS

Great and long-lasting companies know that good business can be achieved in multiple product and service areas. If you neglect to branch out into several different business areas, you are essentially limiting your money-making potential to only what you offer, only to specific customers, and at specific times. This is not to say become a

Jack-Of-All-Trades but to <u>strategically</u> diversify what you do offer and get a bigger piece of the free market pie.

Similarly, to how savvy investors diversify their investment portfolios, diversifying your business offering allows you to balance out your sales strategies to coincide with buyer preferences during various market changes. Also, it is a strategically smart option to offer different products and services that complement your primary business product or service. Staying flexible about what you offer in your products and services ensures that your company will endure changes in the marketplace.

In my consulting business, I quickly realized that "one shoe does not fit all" when it comes down to finding solutions to a business' problem. This has allowed my company to offer various services that we did not originally start our business with. To revise is just fine and that is the way your business should evolve and grow over time. There will be products and services that you begin with, some that you will add, some that you will discontinue, and some that you will alter. All of this is determined by what the market needs and wants in the industry that your business is in.

The only way to continuously provide the greatest value to your clients is to stay educated in what society needs, which is determined by changes in the economy, which influences all aspects of consumer behavior.

CHAPTER ELEVEN

VALUE DRIVEN

See a need, not just a want, and fill that need. Of course, business can be developed from the wants and desires of your clients but on a long-term basis, people will want what they need, not need what they want. This is creating value in its true form. Delivering value will always stand the test of time. Products and services that are simply purchased out of a want are the trendiest of things and have a short lifespan regarding revenue produced.

Having a business that truly provides value must be something that you, the business owner, must understand and can convey that understanding throughout your company. Staff in your company should be able to convey this understanding to your clients. The key point here is that it should not be difficult for the message of value to be explained at any level. This can only be done if the product or service that you provide has a clear and unmistakable sense of value to the end consumer.

I have been involved in several industries where some were based on needs and others were based on wants. Some of these involved sales and others required supporting the customer after the sale. In each situation, selling when the client felt a true need for the product or service was easier. In each situation where selling the product or service and supporting the client after the sale based on a want was far more difficult. Needs based selling is a true business builder as opposed to wants based selling, which is simply a sales goals business.

  At this point, I must say there is a place for most things in the market, even those things that are the trendiest of things; however, the point in this book is to speak to long-term and sustainable business success. Business success has been achieved on wanted trends of the time by certain businesses, but if you truly give thought to many of the companies that achieved long-term success, the true longevity of the company was not one or two products or services, but the company brand itself. Having a solid company brand has allowed many large-scale businesses to enter markets that have been trend based; however, this is not sustainable for smaller and brandless businesses. As a small to medium-sized business owner, the luxury of testing the market without providing true value and without known branding of your business is not business smart and will very much lead to a short lifespan in being in business. The necessity to finding a real consumer need is imperative to being in business for the long-term.

CHAPTER TWELVE
HOW DOES YOUR ORGANIZATIONAL PERFORMANCE IMPACT BUSINESS DEVELOPMENT?

I have seen and been involved in high performing organizations that have lacked the cohesive and satisfied organizational culture that one would think is necessary to highly perform. The goal of making more money and being profitable becomes the only focus of many companies and this is often at the expense of having a satisfied and appreciated workforce.

Developing your business and maintaining satisfied customers will be better accomplished by making sure your internal staff and processes are tended to first. Does high turnover or employees that feel unappreciated have a negative impact on how your external customers are ultimately treated? Of course, this has a tremendous impact and you as a business owner should routinely gauge your employees' emotions to keep your organizational performance exceeding expectations.

Your competitors are constantly looking for experienced talent and headhunters are much obliged to satisfy companies' demands to fill positions. Your experienced business development staff are always in demand and headhunters find these employees great targets because they bring the skills needed to create business. So, in understanding the value of maintaining your workforce, it is easy to see how your business development successes are extremely dependent upon treating your staff well and making them feel appreciated.

There also comes a time when non-performing members of your staff must be dealt with. This can be the most difficult aspect of controlling your organizational culture, but it is very important. Non-performing members of staff often look as though they are performing well; however, the truth is that these team members are the ones that avoid certain tasks, and those tasks are transferred to the "work horses" of your company. This is even more of an issue with inexperienced or non-confrontational management. The overall outcome of this problem is the non-performing "performance look-a-likes" get promoted and the real performing performers look for jobs outside of your company. As a business owner, you will be in a lose / lose situation.

There will come a point where you as a business owner must conduct a staff satisfaction analysis to gauge the moods, priorities, and overall attitudes of your workforce to get a better grasp on your business culture. These types of analyses are typically conducted over a multi-day period where staff are individually spoken to in a relaxed environment. In addition, an analysis can be conducted via online form submittal or "Blind Survey". Both methods result in that some staff prefer one-on-one communication and others feel more relaxed submitting responses through online form submittals.

In addition to analyzing the current state of your workforce the following areas are extremely important to understand.

1. Workforce Needs. Understanding the needs of your workforce in terms of career advancement and tools needed to successfully perform their jobs.
2. Trends In The Workforce. Understanding trends such as generational trends. One age of your workforce will have very different values than other ages in your workforce.
3. Comparative Advantage. Make sure you have the right people doing the right things in your business. If you hire an employee to perform sales in your business but realize that she is better designing online marketing for your website, the comparative advantage would be for her to streamline your online

marketing and increase business exposure through social media.

4. Career Assessment and Career Progression. Always keep the pulse of where your staff are in their careers. If members of your staff are hungry to progress within your business, nurture that hunger and assist them in becoming a more integral part of your company.

5. Importance of Being Humble. Staff that do not possess the humility that you value as a business owner will be a deterrent within your business. Often these types of employees will have a negative impact on the humbler employees that you have working for you.

CHAPTER THIRTEEN

MANAGING YOUR PEOPLE FOR SUCCESS

At every level of your business, leadership must play a role that is conducive of the overall vision of the company. This is extremely important because this also shapes the culture across the company from the front line up to senior management. Managers who manage your sales staff must instill integrity in your salespeople because these are the employees who will be the face and voice of your business each time outside customers are engaged.

As a business owner, you obtain many tools to lead employees early on in your business beginnings. You learn what's needed to treat customers the right way when working directly with them. You also learn to use critical thinking skills when answers to questions aren't easily accessible. These experiences lead to what I consider the main functions of being a high performing manager. The primary functions of any manager are to PLAN, DIRECT, ORGANIZE and CONTROL. A simple way to remember this is PDOC.

Planning involves understanding your staff, which involves their skills and attributes and implementing plans for the business in a manner that the employees' various skills sets align with the business' plan for success. Planning is more than taking a business vision and trying to carry it out. You must have the right people in the right places for proper execution.

After your plan is in place, management must direct the plan to begin moving forward. In the directing role, there must be motivators in place as well as processes to ensure steps are going forward instead of backward to reach specific goals. There will be lessons to learn throughout, so this is where thorough processes need to be in place. On the other hand, during the directing phase, there will be opportunities to realize where specific staff do not fit in the vision of the business so the job of coaching and possibly separation must occur.

As a manager, you will always have to organize your staff to align with the overall vision of your company. This is where having the proper leadership skills come into play. The key here is to always stay on task when specific goals need to be accomplished. Having the ability to organize entails bringing your team together to become stronger instead of members of your team working in silos.

Proper organizational skills also involve keeping your managerial day-to-day duties in focus. Multi-tasking is key when working with your team. You will have varying personalities, backgrounds, experiences, and skills sets among your team members. Managing all members of your team cannot be done the same. Staying flexible as a good manager and leader is a must have.

During the controlling aspect as a manager, you must be aware that the ultimate responsibility of your team rests with you and this includes controlling as much as you can to keep goals in sight and accomplishing these goals while staying aligned with the vision, mission and core values of your business. There are several ways to have managerial control over your team all of which are used differently and at specific times depending on the situation.

The first is making sure the quality of your team's work stays on task. Whether it be sales numbers or customer service standards, controlling your business' outcomes will be well within reach by setting quality standards and having checks in place to realize changes in performance. There are several methods of controlling your staff. I like to focus on what I consider to be the main three, which are setting performance standards, your organizational structure, and having a good quality control process.

IN SUMMARIZATION

To be a long-standing business begins with a solid perceived value of the product or service that you provide. This continues with balancing each step of the process from understanding your core business vision through managing your people with integrity. Business owners that have long-lasting businesses understand their competition but better yet understand themselves and are honest in the path that they want to travel for the overall direction for their company. This involves being very clear about your business talents and what society values in your product or service.

The business vision should be clear, understandable, and concise to the point where you can revisit your vision at any time and be reminded of what your end goal is. It's possible that a vision can be revised to achieve new goals, but the underlying premise should be a continuous benchmark of what your business is striving to accomplish each day and with each transaction.

With each business transaction, your business develops, and this involves having the key personnel in the right positions all of whom have a comparative advantage to successfully contribute to your business. From front-line members of your staff to operational staff, no one position is more important than the other and you, as a business owner, should understand that every link in the chain is dependent upon the next.

In pursuing business, you must be truthful in realizing your key skills and make sure the business that you pursue complements your overall business strategy. Be honest with your staff capabilities and be prepared to do continuous needs assessments to determine where your business is regarding strengths and weaknesses.

Pursuing business means being prepared to negotiate. To some, negotiation means going in with a hardline, which may have been the traditional way of negotiating; however, to foster continued relationships, the proper way to negotiate is to realize the needs on all sides and come to the best satisfying medium. Negotiating should never be a "I got over on them" moment.

During negotiating the relationship begins to strengthen by preparing a contract for success among all parties involved. This entails building long-lasting business through a binding effort. Your contracts should always be viewed as a promise, which should be kept. Your business contracts mean that you were successful at developing business, so always adhere to be a business others can do business with.

Your contracts are also methods to mitigate your risks as a business owner. Risk mitigating should be done daily through your operations. This should always be done on a proactive basis and not an afterthought. Again, having the best staff in the proper positions to mitigate business risk is crucial to your business success.

Understand your competition. Competitiveness is the true essence of having a free market society. Being very clear in what other businesses exist in the market is a must in successfully managing your business. Embrace the idea of always having other businesses looking at what you are doing whether it's through your social media or being in disguise. Always be thoughtful of your interactions with your competitors.

Competitors do not always begin as competition but can once be partners who become competitors. Have a clear understanding that any business partnership can become competition. All business partnerships should have existing confidentiality agreements and proprietary agreements to protect shared information. Protecting your core business ideas and methods is just being business smart.

Being business smart also means innovation. Continuously thinking of your business processes and brainstorming ways to make them better will foster fresh ideas where old ones should be replaced. Think of innovation as you did when first beginning your business, which led to your business strategies and competitiveness. Never be stagnate but always innovate to move forward.

Don't forget the diversification of your business will lead to larger footprints of your business offerings. Having a strategic plan in what you offer as a business owner is important to be flexible to market changes as well as the evolution of your business. Complementing your primary product and service offering with additions over time is imperative to stay abreast of market changes.

Without having real value in what you provide as a business owner will lead to business failure. In providing a valuable product or service, always think of needs instead of simply wants. It will be tempting to start a business based on a trend and trends can be true directions in societal buying; however, always be mindful of the underlying value that you as a business owner provide for business longevity.

As your business grows you will ultimately add staff. Gauging your staff's satisfaction levels while working for you is very important. Disenchanted staff will lead to demotivated staff. Before having a demotivated staff, which causes a decrease in customer satisfaction, it is important to understand your management capabilities or lack thereof.

Management success depends on your management having the ability to plan, direct, organize and control. These are the true responsibilities of leading staff. Understanding your staff, putting plans in place, aligning your staff with the company vision, and reaching goals develops a truly performing team.

Business smarts lead to business success. Be cognizant of your business vision, competitive environment, core business processes, and your internal organization. Your success in being a business professional will only be determined by your abilities and business processes. Only you will truly know when that success has been obtained.

ABOUT THE AUTHOR

Kevin D. Regular, CPCM is a seasoned professional having a broad and long-lasting career in several areas such as finance, insurance, foreign and US government procurement and the oil / gas industry. Mr. Regular has travelled abroad to conduct negotiated transactions as well as become an expert in the field of contract management.

During Mr. Regular's professional career, he has worked on teams as the managing authority to develop new processes and procedures to make business more efficient and profitable. Mr. Regular has worked in world renown organizations in key roles that have solidified his foundation of knowledge in the business arena.

More than a book but a reference for developing business, maintaining business, and successfully managing staff.

Kevin D. Regular, CPCM
Senior Managing Consultant
Rockstone Consulting Group, LLC

www.ingramcontent.com/pod-product-compliance
Lightning Source LLC
Chambersburg PA
CBHW041110180526
45172CB00001B/197